Instar Bible Lessons for toddlers

Jesus Is My Friend

Mary J. Davis

These pages may be copied.

Permission is granted to the buyer of this book to
photocopy student materials for use with
Sunday school or Bible teaching classes.

For information regarding the CPSIA on this printed material call:
203-595-3636 and provide reference # LANC-315751

Rainbow Publishers®

Rainbow Publishers • P.O. Box 261129 • San Diego, CA 92196
www.RainbowPublishers.com

To Larry.

To our children and grandchildren, may God bless each one of you.

INSTANT BIBLE LESSONS FOR TODDLERS: JESUS IS MY FRIEND
©2010 Rainbow Publishers, ninth printing
ISBN 10: 1-58411-036-8
ISBN 13: 978-1-58411-036-1
Rainbow reorder# RB38211
RELIGION / Christian Ministry / Children

Rainbow Publishers
P.O. Box 261129
San Diego, CA 92196
www.RainbowPublishers.com

Cover and Interior Illustrator: Mary Rojas

SUSTAINABLE FORESTRY INITIATIVE

Certified Chain of Custody
Promoting Sustainable
Forest Management
www.sfiprogram.org

Scriptures are from the *Holy Bible: New International Version* (North American Edition), ©1973, 1978, 1984 by the International Bible Society. Used by permission of Zondervan Bible Publishers.

Permission is granted to the buyer of this book to photocopy student materials for use with Sunday school or Bible teaching classes.

All rights reserved. Except as noted above, no part of this publication may be reproduced, stored in a retrieval system, or transmitted in any form or by any means without written permission of Rainbow Publishers.

Printed in the United States of America

■ ■ ■ Contents ■ ■ ■

continued on page 4...

Chapter 9: More Friendly Activities........88

■ ● ■ Introduction ■ ● ■

Do your toddlers know that Jesus is their friend? Knowing that Jesus is our friend is our first step to trusting our Lord for life. After your toddlers participate in the activities in *Jesus Is My Friend*, they will know that our friend Jesus is God's Son, loved to be in God's house, called twelve helpers, made sick people well, taught us how to pray, was praised by the crowd at the Triumphal Entry, and died and rose again. Toddlers will learn to love and trust their special Friend.

Each of the first eight chapters includes a Bible story, memory verse and a variety of activities to help reinforce the truth in the lesson. An additional chapter contains miscellaneous projects that can be used anytime throughout the study or at the end to review the lessons.

The most exciting aspect of *Instant Bible Lessons for Toddlers*, which includes *Growing Up for God*, *God Blesses Me* and *God Takes Care of Me*, is its flexibility. You can easily adapt these lessons to a Sunday school hour, a children's church service, a Wednesday night Bible study or family home use. And because there is a variety of reproducible ideas from which to choose (see below), you will enjoy creating a class session that is best for your group of students, whether large or small, beginning or advanced, active or studious. The intriguing topics will keep your kids coming back for more, week after week.

As toddlers begin to trust Jesus as their friend, they will also grow to trust you, their teacher, as a special friend, too.

✳ How to Use This Book ✳

Each chapter begins with a Bible story which you may read to your class in one of two levels, followed by discussion questions. Following each story page is a story visual for you to make and use as you tell the story. Every story chapter also includes a bulletin board poster with the memory verse and suggestions for using the poster as an activity. All of the activities are tagged with one of the icons below, so you can quickly flip through the chapter and select the projects you need. Simply cut off the teacher instructions on the pages and duplicate!

| craft | teacher help | story visual | action verse | bulletin board | activity |

| puzzle | coloring | song | game | snack |

Chapter 1

My Friend Jesus Is God's Son

Memory Verse

Give him the name Jesus. Luke 1:31

* Story to Share *

2's and 3's ⇝

One day an angel appeared to Mary. The angel said, "Mary, you will have a son. You are to give Him the name Jesus. He will be the Son of God."

Mary and Joseph had to travel to Bethlehem. People everywhere traveled to their hometown to register their names. It was a long trip. Mary's baby would be born any time.

When they arrived in Bethlehem, Joseph looked for a place for them to stay. There was no room at the inn, so they stayed in the stable. Mary's baby was born. She wrapped Him in cloths and placed Him in a manger. Mary gave the baby the name the angel told her to give Him. The baby was named Jesus. Jesus is God's Son.

1's and young 2's ⇝

An angel told Mary, "You will have a baby boy. His name will be Jesus. Jesus will be the Son of God."

Mary and Joseph traveled a long way because they had to go to Bethlehem. In Bethlehem, Mary had her baby boy. There was no room in the inn, so Mary put the baby in a manger. She gave the baby the name the angel had told her: Jesus. Jesus is God's Son.

Based on Luke 1:26-38; 2:1-7

Questions for Discussion

1. What did the angel tell Mary?
2. What was Mary to name the baby?
3. Who's Son is Jesus?

story visual

. . . .

What You Need
- duplicated page
- three pieces of construction paper
- glue

What to Do
1. Cut apart and glue each scene to a sheet of construction paper.
2. As you tell the Bible story from page 7, hold up each scene as it corresponds to the part you are telling.

More Ideas
1. Use the scenes to make a set of story cards for each child. Let the children hold the story cards while you retell the story. Encourage them to look at the pictures and tell the story.
2. Provide dolls and blankets, rockers, baby beds or rugs. Encourage the children to rock their babies, put them to bed or talk to them. Say, **Mary rocked baby Jesus. Baby Jesus took a nap. Baby Jesus was God's Son.**

■ God's Son ■

• Story Cards •

• Bulletin Board Poster •

Give him the name Jesus.
Luke 1:31

Poster Pointer

Fasten the poster onto a bulletin board in your classroom. To make it stand out, mount it onto brightly-colored construction paper, leaving an edge of the construction paper showing. Color the poster with crayons or markers.

What You Need

- pattern on page 10
- construction paper or card stock
- clear, self-stick plastic
- white cloth scraps
- glue

What to Do

1. Depending on how you want to use the poster (see ideas below and at left), enlarge, reduce or simply copy page 10 to fit your bulletin board space.
2. To use the poster as an in-class activity, duplicate the page for each child. Allow them to color the picture. Provide pieces of white cloth for the children to glue onto the baby as a blanket.

■ God's Son ■

Give him the name Jesus.

Luke 1:31

• Good News •
Sing & Rhyme

Good News Rhyme

"Good news," said the angel, "good news."
cup your hands around your mouth

"You are the one God did choose."
point to God

"You will have a baby Son."
rock a pretend baby in your arms

"His name is Jesus. He is God's holy One."
point to God

Good News Song

Mary had a baby boy,

Baby boy,

Baby boy.

Mary had a baby boy,

And Jesus was His name.

What You Need
- duplicated page

What to Do
1. Practice the action rhyme and song before class.
2. Look at the children while you say the "Good News Rhyme" and do the actions. Help them learn the actions.
3. After the children learn the rhyme, teach them the "Good News Song" to the tune of "Mary Had a Little Lamb."
4. If desired, send this page home with the children so their parents can learn the rhyme and song with them.

Toddler Tip
Young children learn through repetition. Do the rhymes and songs more than once when time allows. Use favorite ones at the end for a fun lesson review.

■ God's Son ■

11

puzzle

What You Need
• duplicated page
• crayons

What to Do
1. Help the children find the animals in the stable.
2. Have them color the animals they find. (There are four.)
3. Encourage the children to name each animal they find. Say, **Mary wrapped her baby in cloths and placed Him in a manger. His name was Jesus. Jesus was God's Son.**

• Hidden Picture Puzzle •

Give him the name Jesus.
Luke 1:31

• Baby Jesus Booklet •

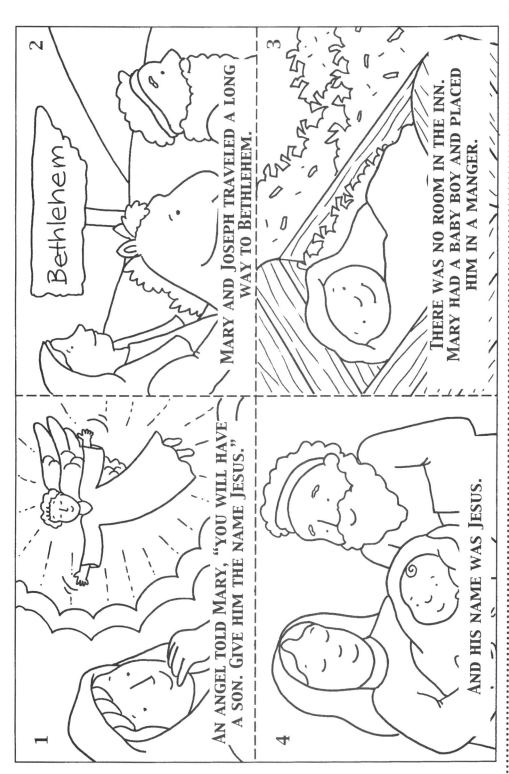

2

Bethlehem

MARY AND JOSEPH TRAVELED A LONG WAY TO BETHLEHEM.

3

THERE WAS NO ROOM IN THE INN. MARY HAD A BABY BOY AND PLACED HIM IN A MANGER.

1

AN ANGEL TOLD MARY, "YOU WILL HAVE A SON. GIVE HIM THE NAME JESUS."

4

AND HIS NAME WAS JESUS.

craft

What You Need
- duplicated page
- construction paper
- crayons
- glue
- stapler

What to Do
1. Before class, cut the illustration into quarters, so each child has four sections for the booklet. Cut sheets of construction paper into quarters, so each child will have four.
2. Allow the children to color the pictures.
3. Help the children glue each picture to a quarter-sheet of construction paper.
4. Arrange the pages from 1 to 4.
5. Staple at the left edge to make a book. (Cover the staples with tape to avoid injury.)
6. Hold up your book and read the phrases as you encourage the children to turn the pages in their own books.

■ God's Son ■

coloring

What You Need
- duplicated page
- crayons

What to Do

1. Hold the picture so the children can see it as you read the story aloud.
2. Allow time for the children to color their pictures.
3. After you read the story, ask the children to share stories of babies they've seen. Ask, **Did you love the baby? Do you love the baby Jesus?**

■ **God's Son** ■

• A New Baby •

Amy smoothed out her new, pink dress. Aunt Janet and Uncle Jim were coming today. They were bringing their new baby for all of the family to see.

"They're here!" Amy's mommy said.

Amy hurried to the door. Aunt Janet was carrying a bundle wrapped in a soft blue blanket. The blanket made a noise! Amy jumped.

Aunt Janet laughed and leaned over to Amy. "Can you see in the blanket?" she asked.

Amy pulled down a piece of the soft, blue blanket. There was a tiny, little baby inside.

"His name is James," Uncle Jimmy said.

Amy went into the kitchen. She took a picture from the front of the refrigerator and brought it to show Aunt Janet and Uncle Jimmy.

"Here is a picture of baby Jesus I colored in Sunday school," she said

"Yes," Aunt Janet said. "Jesus was once a little baby just like baby James."

"I love baby James," Amy said. "And I love baby Jesus."

• Shepherds and •
Angel Ornament

Give him the name Jesus.
Luke 1:31

craft

What You Need
- duplicated page
- tape
- yarn
- crayons

What to Do
1. Duplicate and cut out both star shapes for each child.
2. Help the children match the star shapes and tape them together with the printed sides facing out.
3. Tape a loop of yarn to the top point of the star.
4. Read the memory verse on one side of the star to the children.
5. Say, **After Jesus was born, God sent angels to tell others the Good News!**

■ **God's Son** ■

game

What You Need
• duplicated page

What to Do
1. Cut out the picture and fold it in half at the dashed lines.
2. Staple it to form a two-sided picture.
3. Arrange the children in a circle.
4. Say each child's name, in turn. Point to the child as you say his or her name. Now and then, say "Jesus" and show the picture of Jesus as a baby or Jesus as an adult. Instruct the children to stand and say, "God's Son" each time they hear the name "Jesus" and see Jesus' picture. For example, say, **Jacob, Annie, Kelly, Josh, Jesus. Yes, baby Jesus is God's Son. Brandon, Lauren, Jesus. Yes, Jesus is God's Son.**

• Name Game •

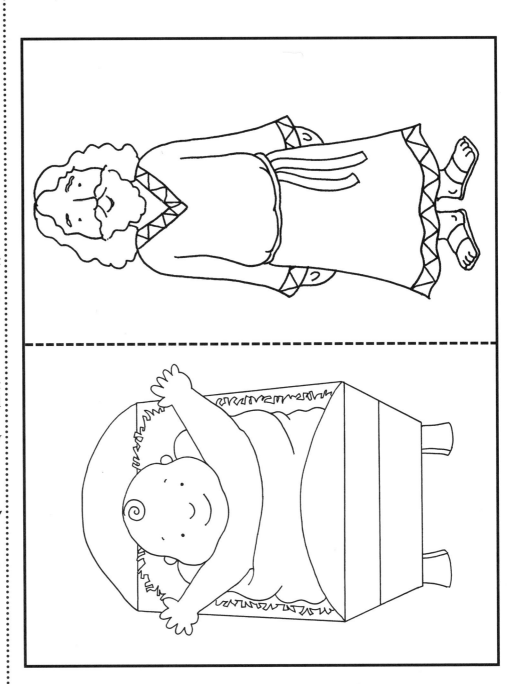

Chapter 2

My Friend Jesus Loves God's House

Memory Verse

I had to be in my Father's house.
Luke 2:49

✶ Story to Share ✶

2's and 3's ⤳

Every year, Mary and Joseph traveled to Jerusalem for the Passover feast. When Jesus was 12, they took Him with them to the feast. It was a long way to travel. Many other families traveled with them.

When the feast was over, the people began to travel home. Joseph and Mary thought Jesus was with them. But when they looked for Him, nobody knew where He was. No one could find Jesus!

Mary and Joseph went back to Jerusalem to look for Jesus. They looked everywhere. They asked people if they had seen Him. They couldn't find Jesus.

After three days, they found Him in the temple with the teachers. Jesus was listening to them teach about God. He asked them questions about God.

Mary said to Jesus, "We were worried about You. Why did You stay here and worry us?"

Jesus answered, "Didn't you know I would be in God's house?"

1's and young 2's ⤳

"Where is Jesus?" Mary and Joseph asked as they looked everywhere. They had traveled a long way to Jerusalem for the Passover feast. But when they had traveled part of the way home, they couldn't find Jesus.

Mary and Joseph went back to Jerusalem to find Jesus. After three days, they found Him. He was in the temple.

"Didn't you know I would be in God's house?" he asked.

Based on Luke 2:41-52

Questions for Discussion

1. Where did Mary and Joseph find Jesus?

2. What did Jesus say to them when they found Him?

story visual

What You Need
- duplicated page
- tape

What to Do

1. Color and cut out the picture. Cut it down the dashed line to make two strips.
2. Tape the two strips together at the 1s and 2s.
3. To tell the story, place the Story-go-round on the table. Turn it in a circle to show the four different scenes as you tell the story.

More Ideas

1. Take the children on a walk around your church. Say, **We are in God's house. This is where we worship. This is where the pastor stands. This is the Sunday school room for older kids.**
2. Let each child hold a Bible. Say, **Jesus wanted to be in God's house and learn about God. We come to God's house to learn from God's Word, too.**

■ God's House ■

• Story-go-round •

• Bulletin Board Poster •

bulletin board

What You Need

- pattern on page 20
- construction paper or card stock
- clear, self-stick plastic
- instant camera and film
- tape

What to Do

1. Depending on how you want to use the poster (see ideas below and at left), enlarge, reduce or simply copy page 20 to fit your bulletin board space.
2. To use the poster as an in-class activity, duplicate the page for each child. Take an instant picture of each child. Tape the picture of the child onto the page. Say, **Brendan is in God's house. Jesus loved to be in God's house, too.**

Poster Pointer

Copy the poster onto card stock for stability. Use colored card stock for effect. Attach the posters onto the wall at the children's eye level to use in review. Or, attach the posters to the wall outside your classroom so parents will be familiar with the lessons the children are learning.

■ God's House ■

I had to be in
my Father's house.
Luke 2:49

• Here They Are •

puzzle

What You Need
- duplicated page
- crayons

What to Do
1. Give each child a duplicated page.
2. Ask, **Where is Jesus?** Help the children connect the dots to complete the temple, then say, **Jesus is in God's house.**
3. Ask, **Where are the boy and girl?** Help the children connect the dots to complete the church, then say, **The boy and girl are in God's house, too.**
4. Read the story to the children. Allow them to color the pictures.

Where is Jesus?
Do you know?
He is lost.
We miss him so.

Mary looked for Jesus.
Joseph looked, too.
They couldn't find Jesus.
What would they do?

They found Him in the temple,
Learning God's Word.
He said, "Don't worry."
"I'm in the house of the Lord."

Jesus loved God's house.
We should love it, too.
God wants us to learn about Him.
For He loves me and you.

■ God's House ■

song

. . . .

What You Need

• duplicated page

What to Do

1. Learn the song to the tune of "Where Is Thumbkin?" and practice the actions before class time.
2. Sing the song and teach the simple actions to the children. Go slowly enough that the children can learn the actions. Repeat several times.

• Where Is Jesus? •

Where is Jesus?

Where is Jesus?

turn palms up

Here I am.

Here I am.

point to self

I love to be in God's house.

I love to be in God's house.

*form roof over head
with hands*

Yes I do.

Yes I do.

shake head yes

• Folding Picture •

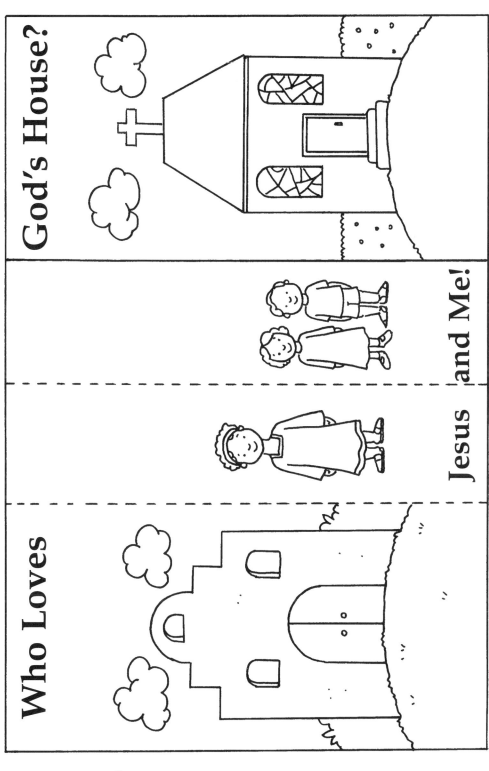

God's House?

Jesus and Me!

Who Loves

What You Need
- duplicated page
- crayons

What to Do
1. Give each child a duplicated page.
2. Allow the children to color the pictures.
3. Help the children fold the picture on the dashed lines.
4. Read the phrases to the children. Ask, **Who loves God's house? Open the picture and see! It's Jesus and me!**

fold on dashed lines

front view folded

■ **God's House** ■

coloring

What You Need
• duplicated page
• crayons

What to Do
1. Hold the picture so the children can see it as you tell the story.
2. After the story give each child a copy.
3. Help the children trace the lines to find the missing objects. Say, **Let's trace the line to find Mommy's purse** [Daddy's keys, boy's shoe, girl's Bible]. **This family is getting ready to go to God's house.** Allow the children to color the pictures.

■ God's House ■

• Getting Ready •

Where is my other shoe?
Where is Mommy's purse?
Daddy can't find his car keys.
My sister is looking for her Bible.
Everyone is getting ready.

Hurry, we might be late!
Where are we going?
We're going to God's house.
We love to go to church!

• Story Puppets •

craft

What You Need
- duplicated page
- toilet tissue tubes
- crayons
- tape

What to Do
1. Before class, cut out the two pictures for each child.
2. While the children color the pictures, say, **This is Mary and Joseph. They are looking for Jesus. This is Jesus. Can you guess where He is? Yes, He's in God's house.**
3. Tape the two pictures onto either side of the top of a tube (the tube makes the pictures easier for small hands to manipulate). Show the children how to turn the tube to show Mary and Joseph, or Jesus and the teachers.

■ God's House ■

game

What You Need
• duplicated page

What to Do
1. Cut out and color the picture of Jesus.
2. Show the picture to the children.
3. Instruct the children to close their eyes while you hide the picture somewhere in the room.
4. Have the children walk around and search for the picture of Jesus. Say, **Jesus is somewhere in God's house. Can you find Jesus?**
5. Repeat if time allows.

■ **God's House** ■

• Find Jesus in • God's House

Chapter 3

My Friend Jesus Loves Children

Memory Verse

Let the little children come to me.
Mark 10:14

✴ Story to Share ✴

2's and 3's ⟿

When Jesus was on earth, mommies and daddies wanted their children to see Him. And they wanted Jesus to touch their children.

"Don't bother Jesus," someone said. "He is busy. Take the children away."

"Stop!" Jesus said. He didn't want the children to go away.

Jesus held out His arms. "Let the little children come to me," He said.

Jesus took some of the children onto His lap. He touched each child and blessed each one. Jesus loves children.

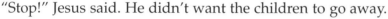

1's and young 2's ⟿

A mommy wanted her little boy to see Jesus but a man said, "No, go away!"

A daddy wanted his little girl to touch Jesus. But another man said, "No, Jesus is busy!"

Many mommies and daddies wanted Jesus to touch their children and bless them.

"Let the children come to Me," Jesus said. He held the children and blessed them. Jesus loves children.

Based on Mark 10:13-16

❓ Questions for Discussion

1. Who did the mommies and daddies want their children to see?

2. What did Jesus say to the ones who wanted to send the children away?

story visual

What You Need
• duplicated page

What to Do
1. Cut out Jesus and the four children.
2. Fold Jesus on the dashed lines to form a "lap" as shown.
3. To tell the story, set the Jesus figure on the table. As you tell the story, place the children, one by one, in Jesus' lap.

More Ideas
1. Provide dolls for the children to hold and hug. Say, **Jesus liked to hold the children on His lap. Jesus loves children.**
2. Sing, "Jesus Loves the Little Children." Display a picture of Jesus while the children sing the song. Instruct the children to hug themselves every time they hear the word "Jesus" in the song.

■ **Loves** ■
Children

• Story Lap •

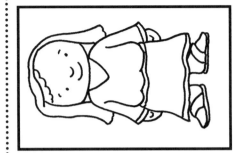

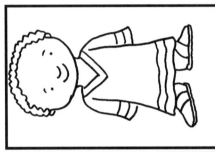

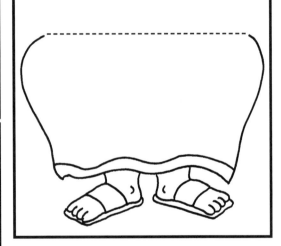

folded story lap

• Bulletin Board Poster •

bulletin board
· · · · · · · · · · ·
What You Need
- pattern on page 30
- construction paper or card stock
- clear, self-stick plastic
- instant camera and film

What to Do
1. Depending on how you want to use the poster (see ideas below and at left), enlarge, reduce or simply copy page 30 to fit your bulletin board space.
2. To use the poster as an in-class activity, make a "Jesus loves the children" bulletin board. Take instant photos of the children, or ask for photos from their parents. Attach the children's photos to the bulletin board around the picture of Jesus. Show each child his or her picture on the bulletin board. Say, **Jesus loves all the little children. Jesus loves Nicholas** [mention each name].

Poster Pointer

Make the poster durable by covering it with clear, self-stick plastic. Let each child hold a covered poster. While the children are holding the posters, say the memory verse together several times.

■ **Loves** ■
Children

29

Let the little children come to me.

Mark 10:14

• Arms Open Wide •

"Let the little children come to Me."
Jesus held His arms out wide.
"I like nothing better than holding
little children by My side."

What You Need
- duplicated page
- crayons

What to Do
1. Give a copy of the page to each child.
2. Help the children trace the lines to finish drawing some of the children running to Jesus.
3. Help the children draw Jesus' arms.
4. Read the verse to the children.

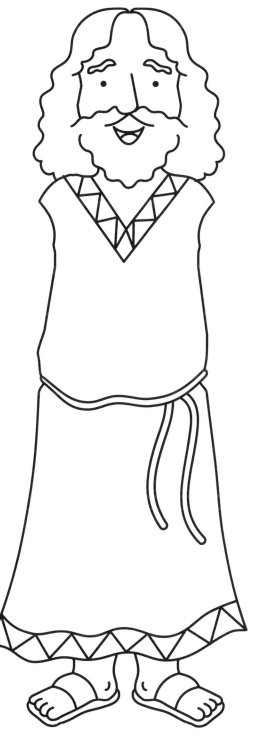

■ **Loves** ■
Children

What You Need
• duplicated page

What to Do
1. Practice the "Hug, Hug" verse and actions before class.
2. Show the children how to hug themselves.
3. Say the verse with the children.
4. After saying the verse several times, teach the "Praise Chant" to the children. Each time you repeat the chant together, get louder and louder.

• Hugs •

Hug, Hug

Hug, hug.
Jesus hugged the children.

hug self

Hug, hug,
And they hugged Him back.

hug self

teacher hugs child

Hug, hug.
I can hug the children.

teacher hugs another child

Hug, hug.
Will you hug me back?

Praise Chant

Whom does Jesus love?
Jesus loves ME!
Whom does Jesus love?
Jesus loves YOU!

Who loves Jesus?
I love Jesus!
Who loves Jesus?
You love Jesus!

■ **Loves** ■
Children

• Springy Shapes •

craft

. . . .

What You Need

- duplicated page
- plain paper
- glue

What to Do

1. Before class, cut the Jesus scene from the page, cut out the picture shapes and cut four 4" paper strips for each child.
2. Help the children fold the paper strips accordion-style.
3. Show how to glue a folded strip to the back of each shape and how to glue the other end of the folded strip to the matching shape on the page. (For very young children, tape a paper spring to the back of each figure before class.)
4. Say, **Jesus loves children. Jesus loves me and you!**

■ Loves ■ Children

33

coloring

What You Need
- duplicated page
- Bible stickers
- crayons

What to Do
1. Color the picture.
2. Hold up a copy of it so all of the children can see it as you tell the story.
3. Afterward, allow time for the children to color their pictures.
4. Let the children add Bible stickers to their pictures. Say, **Jake's mommy read the story about Jesus from the Bible. The Bible tells us that Jesus loved the little children.**

• Glad to See You •

Jake went to the window and looked out. "Daddy isn't home yet," he said.

A few minutes later, Jake looked out the window again. "Daddy isn't home yet," he said.

Mommy put some cookies and a glass of milk on the table. "Let's have a little snack while we wait for Daddy to come home," she said.

Mommy opened her Bible and read a story to Jake.

"Jesus' helpers saw some children coming close. 'Send them away,' the helpers said. 'Jesus is too busy for children.'

"Jesus saw the children and said, 'Wait! Let the children come to Me.' Jesus held the children and hugged them." Mommy closed her Bible.

Soon, the door opened. Daddy barely got inside the door when Jake jumped into his arms. "I am so glad to see you," Jake said.

Daddy hugged him tightly. "I am glad to see you, too," Daddy said.

Mommy smiled. "Just like Jesus was glad to see the children," she said.

• A Hug from Jesus •

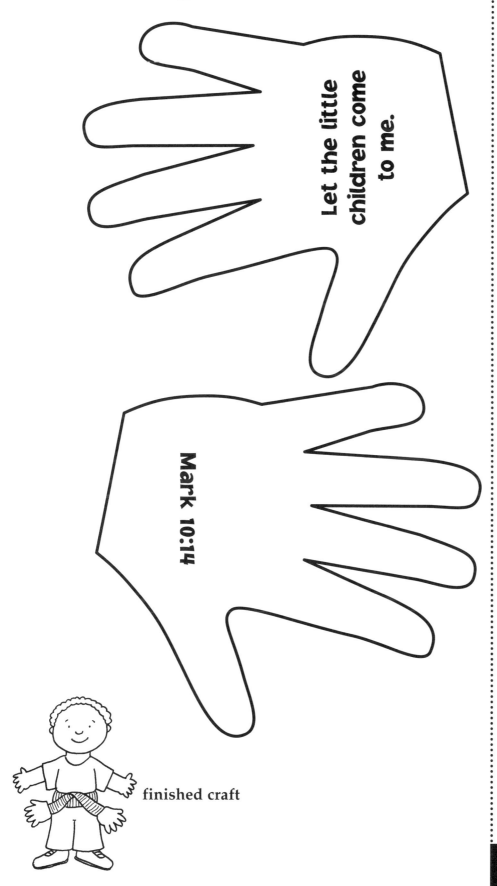

Let the little children come to me.

Mark 10:14

finished craft

craft

. . . .

What You Need

• duplicated page
• crepe paper
• tape

What to Do

1. Before class, cut out a pair of hands for each child and cut crepe paper into 2½-foot lengths, one per child.
2. Help the children tape one hand shape to each end of the crepe paper.
3. Tie the crepe paper loosely around the child's waist. Say, **We are wrapping Jesus' arms around you for a great big hug!**

■ **Loves** ■
Children

35

activity

What You Need
- duplicated page
- tape
- boom box
- cassette or CD

What to Do
1. Tape a picture of Jesus onto the front of a chair-back for each child. Make sure the picture of Jesus shows from the front so it looks like the chair is Jesus' lap. Have some extra pictures ready in case you have more children than planned.
2. Arrange the chairs in a line or circle. Make sure there are enough chairs for each child to sit down.
3. Arrange the children in a circle around the chairs.
4. Turn on the music and help the children walk in a circle around the chairs (as in "Musical Chairs").
5. Turn off the music and help each child find a chair to sit in.
6. Say, **We are sitting in Jesus' lap. Our friend Jesus loves children.**

■ Loves ■ Children

• Jesus' Lap •

Chapter 4

My Friend Jesus Calls Helpers

Memory Verse

"Follow me," Jesus said. Mark 1:17

* Story to Share *

2's and 3's ↝

Jesus needed some helpers. He needed people who would follow Him wherever He went and help Him teach people about God and heaven.

Jesus walked beside the Sea of Galilee. There He saw Simon Peter and his brother Andrew throwing a fish net into the lake. They were fishermen.

Jesus said to Peter and Andrew, "Come, follow Me. I will make you fishers of men." Peter and Andrew left their fishing nets and followed Jesus.

Later, Jesus saw James and his brother John fixing their fishing nets in a boat. Jesus called them to be His helpers, too.

Another day, Jesus saw Matthew collecting taxes. "Follow Me," Jesus said. Matthew left his tax table. All together, Jesus called 12 people to be His helpers. Their names were: Peter, Andrew, James, John, Philip, Bartholomew, Matthew, Thomas, James, Thaddaeus, Simon and Judas.

1's and young 2's ↝

Jesus needed some helpers. He saw Peter and Andrew getting ready to catch some fish. "Come, follow Me," Jesus said.

Then Jesus saw James and John. "Follow Me," He told them.

Jesus found Matthew sitting at a tax collector's table. "Follow Me," Jesus said. Matthew followed Him right away.

Jesus called 12 helpers.

Based on Mark 1:16-20; 2:13-17; 3:13-19

Questions for Discussion

1. What were Peter, Andrew, James and John doing before Jesus called them?
2. What did Jesus tell Peter and Andrew they would become?
3. How many people did Jesus call to be His helpers?

story visual

What You Need
• this page and page 39, duplicated
• tape

What to Do
1. Cut out all three numbered sections.
2. Place the sections in a long strip with the numbers counting down from 1 to 12.
3. Tape the strips together.
4. To tell the story, hold the strip off the table. Begin with number 1, and point to each picture as you tell of that disciple.
5. Then start at the top of the chart and say each number and name. Have the children follow the counting with their fingers.

Another Idea
Show older toddlers that Jesus calls each of us. Say each disciple's name and have the children beckon each disciple. Say, Jesus said to Peter, "Follow Me." Repeat with each name. Then do the same with each child's name.

■ Calls ■
Helpers

• Counting Chart •

5 MATTHEW

6 PHILIP

7 BARTHOLOMEW

8 THOMAS

9 JAMES

10 THADDAEUS

11 SIMON

12 JUDAS

bulletin board

What You Need
- pattern on page 41
- construction paper or card stock
- clear, self-stick plastic

What to Do
1. Depending on how you want to use the poster (see ideas below and at right), enlarge, reduce or simply copy page 41 to fit your bulletin board space.
2. To use the poster as an in-class activity, give each child a copy of the page. Turn the page over and trace one or both of the child's footprints on the page. Say, **We can use our feet to follow Jesus.**

■ **Calls** ■
Helpers

• Bulletin Board Poster •

Poster Pointer

Copy the poster, then copy a letter to parents on the back with classroom updates such as the week's memory verse, a report on the child's good and bad behavior, supply needs and so on.

"Follow me," Jesus said.

Mark 1:17

puzzle

What You Need

- duplicated page
- crayons
- washable paint
- paint smocks
- shallow pans
- thin sponges

What to Do

1. Before class, cut several foot shapes from sponges. Pour thin layers of paint into the shallow pans.
2. Give each child a copy of this page. Help the children into paint smocks.
3. Place a shallow pan of paint in the reach of every three or four children.
4. Help the children press the sponge footprints into the paint, then onto the page making footprints from Jesus to the disciples. Say, **Jesus said, "Follow Me."**
5. Read the story from page 37 again to the children as they work.

■ **Calls** ■
Helpers

• Follow Me •

JESUS

• Follow Jesus •

Follow Jesus

We put our left foot in,
We put our left foot out,
We put our left in and shake it
all about.
We can follow Jesus, let's turn
ourselves around.
That's what it's all about.

song/verse

What You Need
• duplicated page
• rope or hula hoop

What to Do
1. Sing "Follow Jesus" to the tune of "The Hokey Pokey" with the children, adding body parts as desired: arm, foot, head, etc. Place a rope circle or hula hoop on the floor so the children can visualize putting their feet and other body parts in and out.
2. Say the "Counting Rhyme." Help the children hold up the correct number of fingers for each number.
3. Sing "Follow" to the tune of "Good Night, Ladies." Wave toward yourself to indicate "follow me" as you lead the children around the room.

Counting Rhyme

One, two, three,
Jesus said, "Follow Me."
Four, five, six.
Then more men He picks.
Seven, eight, nine,
To help Him all the time.
Ten, eleven, twelve, that's all.
The 12 men followed Jesus' call.

Follow

Follow Jesus,
Follow Jesus,
Follow Jesus.
Jesus said, "Follow Me."

■ Calls ■
Helpers

craft

What You Need

- duplicated page
- shoebox lids
- glue
- rickrack or other trim
- hole punch
- yarn

What to Do

1. Allow each child to color a picture of Jesus.
2. Help each child glue a picture of Jesus in the center of the shoebox lid.
3. Help the children glue rickrack or another trim around the edge of the picture.
4. Punch two holes in the lid and add a loop of yarn for hanging the plaque.

• Follow Jesus Plaque •

FOLLOW

JESUS

MARK 1:17

finished craft

■ Calls ■ Helpers

• I Can Follow Jesus •

puzzle

What You Need
- duplicated page
- crayons

What to Do
1. Hold a copy of the page so all of the children can see it as you read the rhyming story.
2. Afterward, give each child a copy of the page.
3. Help the children find the hidden items and color them: church, Bible, heart, praying hands.
4. As they work, say, **We follow Jesus when we go to church. Can you find a church? We follow Jesus when we read our Bible. Can you find a Bible?** Repeat with heart and praying hands.

I can follow Jesus
There are many ways.
I can go to church
To worship God on Sundays.

I can follow Jesus
To learn about our Lord.
I can have my parents help me
To study in God's Word.

I can follow Jesus
By always helping others.
I can share His love
With my friends, my sisters, my brothers.

I can follow Jesus
Each and every day.
One good way to follow Him
Is to always take time to pray.

■ Calls ■
Helpers

snack

What You Need

- duplicated page
- crayons
- paper or foam cups
- tape
- plastic spoons
- goldfish crackers

What to Do

1. Cut out a strip for each child.
2. Allow the children to color the lettering.
3. Help the children to tape the strip to a cup.
4. Give each child a spoon.
5. Place shallow containers of goldfish crackers so every child can reach one.
6. While the children spoon crackers into their cups, say, **Jesus called some fishermen to be His followers. Jesus said to them, "Follow Me."**

■ **Calls** ■
Helpers

• Fish Snacks •

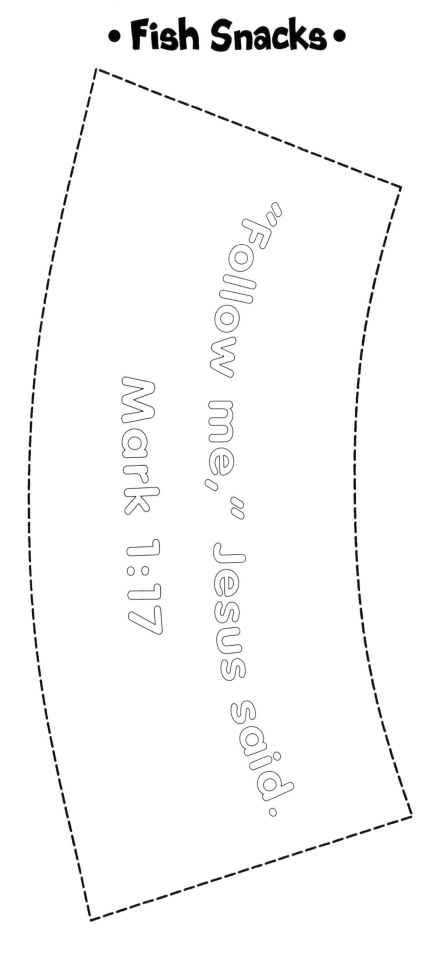

"Follow me," Jesus said.

Mark 1:17

Chapter 5

My Friend Jesus Makes People Well

Memory Verse

He healed them. Luke 4:40

* Story to Share *

2's and 3's ⟿

Jesus and His helpers traveled all around. Jesus taught people about God. He was God's Son.

Wherever Jesus went, people came to Him to be healed. Sick people came to Jesus because they knew He could make them well. People with broken legs came to Jesus because they knew He could make them walk again. Blind and deaf people came to Jesus because they knew He could make them see and hear again.

One day, Jesus went to Peter's home. Peter's mother-in-law was sick. Jesus touched her and made her well.

People came to Jesus all day. Jesus touched the people, one by one, and made them well.

1's and young 2's ⟿

Jesus traveled all over. He told people about God. He made sick people well.

One day, Peter's mother-in-law was sick. Jesus went into the house and made her well again.

Many people came to Jesus to be made well. Jesus touched the people and they weren't sick anymore.

Based on Luke 4

Questions for Discussion

1. Why did sick people go to Jesus?

2. What did Jesus do when Peter's mother-in-law was sick?

story visual

What You Need
• duplicated page
• paper fastener

What to Do
1. Color and cut out the scene.
2. Color and cut out the Jesus figure.
3. Poke a paper fastener through the hole in the Jesus figure and the indicated hole on the scene.
4. To tell the story, tip forward the Jesus figure to show how Jesus touched many people to make them well.

Another Idea
Bring pictures of medical items (ads often feature these images) and some actual items. Show the pictures and items. Say, **When we are sick, a doctor takes care of us. Doctors have many ways to make us well, such as medicine. Jesus made many people well. But He only had to speak or to touch someone, and that person became well. Jesus is God's Son.**

■ Makes ■ People Well

• Healing Touch •

Jesus

• Bulletin Board Poster •

What You Need

- pattern on page 50
- construction paper or card stock
- clear, self-stick plastic
- bandages

What to Do

1. Depending on how you want to use the poster (see ideas below and at left), enlarge, reduce or simply copy page 50 to fit your bulletin board space.

2. To use the poster as an in-class activity, duplicate the page for each child. Let the children place an adhesive bandage on the picture to remind them that Jesus made people well.

Poster Pointer

Copy the poster and tape several onto a table. Cover the table with removable clear plastic and provide crayons for a before class coloring activity. Wipe off crayon marks with a damp cloth after class to provide a clean surface for the following week.

■ Makes ■ People Well

He healed them.

Luke 4:40

• Hands That Heal •

He healed them.
~ Luke 4:40

activity

What You Need
• duplicated page
• crayons

What to Do
1. Read the story on page 47 to the children while showing them the picture.
2. Afterward, give each child a copy of the page.
3. Help the children trace the broken lines to draw the handprints.
4. Say, **Jesus touched the sick people with His hands. Then they became well.**

■ **Makes** ■
People Well

51

song/verse

What You Need

• duplicated page

What to Do

1. Sing "Jesus Made Many People Well" with the children to the tune of "Wheels on the Bus." As you lead the song, put your hands on each of the children.

2. Next, do the action rhyme. Slowly teach each action to the children so they will understand what to do.

• Jesus Made People Well •

Jesus Made Many People Well

Jesus went around making people well,
People well,
People well.
Jesus went around making people well,
All through the town.

"Thank You, Jesus," the people said,
People said,
People said.
"Thank You, Jesus," the people said,
All through the town.

Jesus Touched

Touch, touch, touch.
Jesus touched a blind man's eyes.

touch eyes

Touch, touch, touch.
Jesus touched a deaf man's ears.

touch ears

Touch, touch, touch.
Jesus made all the sick people well.

touch tummy

■ Makes ■ People Well

• Jesus Touched Them •

Luke 4:40

finished craft

Luke 4:40

craft

What You Need
• duplicated page
• hole punch
• yarn
• tape

What to Do
1. Before class, cut out a Jesus figure and pair of hands for each child. Punch a hole in each shoulder of the Jesus figure where indicated. Cut a 1-foot length of yarn for each child.
2. Allow the children to color the Jesus figure.
3. Help the children thread the yarn through the holes from the back.
4. Center and tape the yarn in the back at center.
5. Allow the children to tape a hand to each end of the yarn.
6. Show the children how to "touch" someone with Jesus' hands. Say, **Jesus touched the sick people and made them well.**

■ **Makes** ■
People Well

coloring

What You Need
- duplicated page
- crayons

What to Do
1. Hold up a copy of the picture so the children can see it as you read the story below.
2. Afterward, while the children color their pictures, ask, **Do you know someone who is sick? We can pray for that person so Jesus will help him or her get well.**

■ **Makes** ■
People Well

• Helping Someone Get Well •

Michael held tightly to the pretty bouquet of flowers. Mommy let him pick out the red and pink flowers all by himself. Aunt Lee would be happy to get the pretty flowers.

"Here we are," Mommy said. She helped Michael get out of the car with the big bouquet of flowers.

"Oh," Aunt Lee said. She hugged Michael. "I love these pretty flowers. It's not fun being sick, but you have helped me feel much better."

Michael sat on a chair. "We learned in Sunday school how Jesus made people well. I have been praying that you would feel better soon."

"Thank you for praying for me," Aunt Lee said. "And thank you for bringing me flowers."

Michael liked knowing he helped. Only Jesus can make people well, but Michael helped Aunt Lee feel better by bringing her something pretty.

• Feel Better Card •

I hope
you feel
better
soon!

He healed them.
~ Luke 4:40

craft

. . . .

What You Need
- duplicated page
- crayons

What to Do
1. Cut out a card for each child.
2. Help the children fold the card on the dashed lines.
3. While the children color their cards, say, **We can help others feel better when they are sick by giving them a card and praying for them. To whom will you give your card?**
4. Help each child write his or her name on the card.

■ Makes ■
People Well

• Clay Hands •

craft

. . . .

What You Need

• lunch sacks or containers
• items for recipe (at right)

What to Do

1. Before class, make the clay dough. Wash the classroom tables for a clean play surface.
2. Give each child some dough. Show how to smooth it out.
3. Help the children press their hands in the dough to make a hand print.
4. Say, **Jesus used His hands to touch people and make them well.**
5. If the children want to keep their handprints, place them inside a paper lunch sack or airtight container to carry home. If not, keep the dough in an airtight container to use for other activities with the children.

■ **Makes** ■
People Well

Safe Clay Dough

1 cup flour

½ cup salt

2 teaspoons cream of tartar

1 tablespoon cooking oil

1 cup water

food coloring

1. Mix the dry ingredients.

2. Stir in the oil and water.

3. Add a few drops of food coloring to make desired shade.

4. Cook the dough over medium heat, stirring continuously with a wooden spoon. Cook until the dough clings together.

5. Cool, then turn out onto a floured surface and knead until the dough is the desired consistency.

6. Store in airtight container.

Yield: suitable for 4 or 5 children

Chapter 6

My Friend Jesus Teaches Us How to Pray

Memory Verse

Pray to your Father. Matthew 6:6

* Story to Share *

2's and 3's ⤳

Jesus taught people all around Him. He told them about heaven. He taught people how to be children of God. He even taught people how to pray.

"Don't be like some," Jesus said. "Don't pray really loud just to make noise. Pray to God the Father. He knows what you need before you even ask Him."

Jesus said a prayer to show the people how to pray. Then He told the people to forgive others, just as God had forgiven them.

That is how Jesus wants us to pray.

1's and young 2's ⤳

Jesus sat on a hillside so all the people could see Him. Many people came to listen to Jesus. "This is how to pray," Jesus said. "Talk to God the Father."

Jesus said a prayer to show how to pray. He also told the people that they should forgive each other, just like God had forgiven them.

Based on Matthew 6:5-13

? Questions for Discussion

1. Who taught the people how to pray?

2. Whom should we pray to?

3. What does God know even before we ask Him?

story visual

What You Need
- this page and page 59, duplicated
- tape

What to Do
1. Color and cut apart the strips on this page. Color and cut out the picture on page 59.
2. Lay the two story sections on top of the full section. Tape on either side so the half-sections open to reveal the one underneath.
3. To tell the story, show the main scene where Jesus is teaching (fold the two flaps to the back). As you tell about the two men praying in different ways, fold the smaller flaps to the front so that they show.

Another Idea
Play a game in which the children copy what you do. Pray in different ways, such as sitting, standing, holding hands with others, etc. Say, **Jesus taught the people how to pray.**

■ **Teaches** ■
How to Pray

• Hinged Picture •

tape here

tape here

• Bulletin Board Poster •

bulletin board

· · · · · · · · · · ·

What You Need

- pattern on page 61
- construction paper or card stock
- clear, self-stick plastic
- glue
- praying hands stickers
- yarn

What to Do

1. Depending on how you want to use the poster (see ideas below and at right), enlarge, reduce or simply copy page 61 to fit your bulletin board space.

2. To use the poster as an in-class activity, duplicate the page for each child. Have the children glue a copy of the page to the center of a sheet of construction paper. Give the children some praying hands stickers to attach to the picture. Add a loop of yarn to the picture for a hanger.

Poster Pointer

Copy each poster to card stock, one for each child. Punch holes in eight or 10 places around the edge of the card. Put a small piece of tape around the end of a one-yard length of yarn for easy lacing. Let the children lace the cards. Say the memory verse several times while the children are working and encourage them to say it with you.

■ Teaches ■
How to Pray

Pray to your father.

Matthew 6:6

puzzle

What You Need
- duplicated page
- crayons

What to Do

1. Say, **The people are climbing on the mountain to listen to Jesus. Help the people find Jesus on the mountain.**

2. Help the children draw a line through the maze to have the people reach Jesus.

3. While the children color their pictures, read the Lord's Prayer to them. Say, **This is the prayer Jesus taught the people to say.**

• Climb the Mountain •

Our Father who art in heaven, hallowed be Thy name. Thy kingdom come, Thy will be done on earth as it is in heaven. Give us this day our daily bread. And forgive us our trespasses, as we forgive those who trespass against us. And lead us not into temptation, but deliver us from evil.

— paraphrased from Matthew 6:9-13

• This Is How to Pray •

This Is How to Pray

Jesus said, "This is how to pray."
It's good to talk to God each day.
Thank Him, praise Him, say "I love You."
Tell God you know He loves you, too.
Jesus said, "This is how to pray."
It's good to talk to God each day.

I Love to Pray

I love to pray,
I love to pray,
I love to pray,
To my Father above.

When Jesus Taught

The people listened with their ears.

touch ears

They watched Him with their eyes.

point upward

When Jesus taught the people,

touch eyes

They knew He was very wise.

touch head with index finger

What You Need
• duplicated page

What to Do
1. Sing the songs with the children. Sing "This Is How to Pray" to the tune of "Twinkle, Twinkle Little Star." Sing "I Love to Pray" to the tune of "God Is So Good."
2. Practice doing the action verse with the actions. Help the children do each action as you repeat the verse. Do it a few times together so the children can learn the actions and try to say the verse.

■ Teaches ■
How to Pray

craft

What You Need
- duplicated page
- crayons
- tape

What to Do
1. Allow the children to color the pictures.
2. Help the children fold the page on the dashed lines to form a triangle. Tape at the seam.
3. Show how to turn the prayer triangle to show the different times of day we can pray.

• Prayer Triangle •

I pray in the morning.

I pray at night.

I pray when I eat.

• Talking to God •

coloring

What You Need
• duplicated page
• crayons

What to Do
1. Hold up a copy of the page so the children can see the picture as you tell the story at left.
2. Afterward, allow the children to color the picture.
3. As the children work, say, **It's easy to pray. We just talk to God, our Father.**

At home after church, Brianna told Mommy, "I can't pray out loud in Sunday school. I don't know what to say."

Mommy smiled and hugged Brianna. "A prayer is just talking to God," she said. "Let's read about it in the Bible."

Mommy opened her Bible and read a verse. "Jesus said, 'When you pray…pray to your Father.'"

Brianna bowed her head. "God, I thought it would be hard to pray at Sunday school. But now I know it's easy. I can just talk to You about whatever I want."

Brianna was very happy that she could talk to God.

■ **Teaches** ■
How to Pray

craft

What You Need
- duplicated page
- glue
- crayons

What to Do
1. Before class, cut out a door hanger and a boy or girl for each child.
2. Help the children color the door hanger and glue on a boy or girl.
3. Say, **The children are praying before they go to sleep. God likes for us to talk to Him.**
4. Show how to hang the door hanger on a doorknob.

• Bedtime Door Hanger •

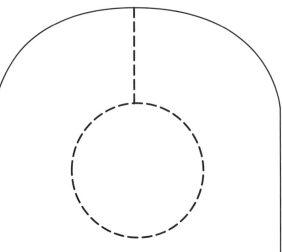

As I go to bed each night, I will pray to God.

Pray to your Father.
~ Matthew 6:6

Chapter 7

We Praise My Friend Jesus

Memory Verse

Hosanna!...Blessed is the King!
John 12:13

* Story to Share *

2's and 3's ⟿

There were many people in Jerusalem. It was time for them to come to the Passover feast.

When the people heard that Jesus was coming to Jerusalem, they were very excited. Some cut palm branches to wave. Many people lined up along the streets to see Jesus.

Soon, Jesus rode into the city on a donkey. The people shouted, "Hosanna! Blessed is the King!" They praised Jesus and waved the palm branches. Then they shouted some more, "Hosanna! Blessed is the King!"

1's and young 2's ⟿

The people in Jerusalem heard that Jesus was coming there soon. They were so excited! They lined up along the streets and waited.

Soon, Jesus came into the city, riding on a donkey. The people waved palm branches at Him and praised Him.

"Hosanna!" the people shouted. "Blessed is the King!"

Based on John 12:12-15

Questions for Discussion

1. What did people wave when Jesus came into town?
2. What did the people shout?
3. Who is the King?
4. What was Jesus riding on?

story visual

What You Need
• duplicated page
• green construction paper

What to Do
1. Before class, cut out and color the picture. Cut a few palm leaves from green paper.
2. Fold the picture in half at the dashed lines.
3. As you tell the story, move the Jesus stand-up along the table. Place some palm leaves on the table close to Jesus.
4. Allow the children to make their own Jesus figure and reenact the story with you.

Another Idea
Attach a length of crepe paper to the front of each donkey. Let the children pull their donkeys around the room. Say, **Jesus came to Jerusalem riding on a donkey. The people praised Him.**

■ **We Praise** ■

• Praising Jesus •

• Bulletin Board Poster •

What You Need
- pattern on page 70
- construction paper or card stock
- clear, self-stick plastic

What to Do
1. Depending on how you want to use the poster (see ideas below and at left), enlarge, reduce or simply copy page 70 to fit your bulletin board space.
2. To use the poster as an in-class activity, duplicate the page for each child. Cut palm leaves from green paper for them to glue onto the picture.

Poster Pointer

Make one or more copies of the unit poster book (see instructions on page 89). Keep the books visible for children to "read."

▪ We Praise ▪

69

Hosanna!...Blessed is the King!
John 12:13

• Jesus Is Coming! •

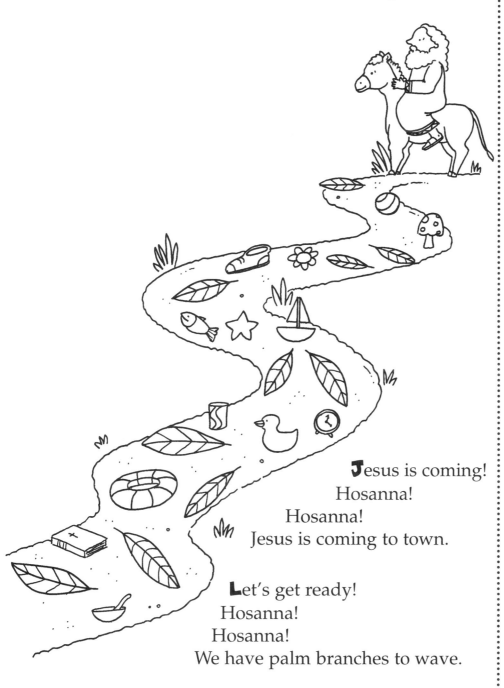

coloring

What You Need
• duplicated page
• crayons

What to Do
1. Instruct the children to color green only the palm leaves.
2. While they are coloring, tell the rhyming story.

Jesus is coming!
Hosanna!
Hosanna!
Jesus is coming to town.

Let's get ready!
Hosanna!
Hosanna!
We have palm branches to wave.

Shout to Jesus!
Hosanna!
Hosanna!
Jesus is the King!

■ **We Praise** ■

song/verse

What You Need
• duplicated page

What to Do
1. Sing "Praise and Sing" with the children to the tune of "Three Blind Mice." Clap your hands together when you get to that verse in the song.
2. Teach "Here Comes" to the children. Have them tap their feet and clap their hands as they repeat the verse with you.

• Praise and Sing •

Praise and Sing

Praise and sing,
Praise and sing.
Jesus is King,
Jesus is King.
We lift our voices to praise Him,
We sing our songs to praise Him,
We clap our hands to praise Him.
Praise and sing.
Jesus is King.

Here Comes

Clop, clop, clop.
Here comes the donkey.

tap feet on floor

Clap clap clap
Here comes Jesus, too.

clap hands

• Spinning Praiser •

Hosanna!...Blessed is the King!

~ John 12:13

What You Need
- duplicated page
- paper towel tubes
- green construction paper
- tape

What to Do

1. Before class, duplicate and cut out the verse strip from the page for each child. Cut four 1" x 11" strips of green paper for each child.
2. Show how to tape one strip of green paper to four places along the top edge of the tube. Bend each strip back a little, so they point outward.
3. Show how to tape the verse strip around the tube, about halfway up.
4. Show the children how to roll the tube in their hands to make it spin. Say, **See how the praiser spins? We can use our spinning praisers to praise Jesus.**

■ **We Praise** ■

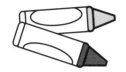

coloring

What You Need
• duplicated page
• crayons

What to Do
1. Show the children the illustration as you read the story to them. Ask, **How can we praise Jesus?**
2. Afterward, allow time for them to color the pictures.

• Twin Praise •

Sarah and Susan were twin sisters. They did many things the same way.

Sarah held her Bible tightly. "I can praise Jesus by taking my Bible to church," she said.

Susan held her Bible tightly, too. "I can praise Jesus by taking my Bible to church, too," she said.

"I can sing to Jesus in church," Sarah said.

"I can sing to Jesus in church, too," Susan said.

"Well, I can pray and praise Jesus," Sarah said.

"Me, too," said Susan. "I can pray and praise Jesus, too." Mom laughed.

"Okay, you two," Mom said. "You can both praise Jesus in a lot of ways. Even though you two look alike, Jesus wants to hear from both of you. He loves to hear everyone's praise."

• Praise Puzzle •

puzzle

What You Need
• duplicated page
• crayons
• letter envelopes
• clear, self-stick plastic

What to Do
1. As the children color the picture, read the Scripture to them.
2. Cover the puzzles with clear, self-stick plastic and cut them apart at the dashed lines.
3. Help the children reassemble their puzzles.
4. Give each child an envelope to carry home the puzzle.

Hosanna!...Blessed is the King!
~ John 12:13

■ We Praise ■

snack

What You Need

• plastic drinking straws
• miniature marshmallows
• round cereal pieces
• beverages

What to Do

1. Give each child a straw. Provide mini-marshmallows and round cereal pieces.
2. Help the children make "kabobs" by threading on a marshmallow and then a piece of cereal, and repeating until the straw is filled.
3. While the children work, say, **Let's say a way to praise Jesus each time we put something on our straws.** Suggest: praying, singing, giving, going to church, being kind, helping others, obeying parents, sharing with others, telling others about Jesus, etc.
4. Repeat some of the ideas until the children have filled their straws. Enjoy!

■ We Praise ■

• Praise Kabobs •

Chapter 8

My Friend Jesus Died and Rose Again

Memory Verse

He has risen. Matthew 28:6

✳ Story to Share ✳

2's and 3's →

Jesus was God's Son. Many people believed it, but some didn't. Those who didn't believe wanted to get rid of Jesus. They arrested Jesus and put Him on a cross to die.

After He died, Jesus was placed in a tomb. A big stone was rolled in front of the tomb. Soldiers guarded the tomb.

When some women came to see the tomb, they saw that the stone had been rolled away. And an angel was sitting inside!

"Good news!" the angel said. "Jesus is not here! He has risen!" Jesus was alive again.

The angel told the women to go to Galilee and they would find Jesus there. As they were on their way, someone said to them, "Greetings."

It was Jesus! The women were so happy to see Him! They bent down and held His feet to worship Him.

Jesus said, "Go and tell the others to go to Galilee. There they will see Me."

1's and young 2's →

Jesus was God's Son. Many people knew it. But some people didn't believe it.

Those who didn't believe it had Jesus put in jail. Jesus was put on a cross to die. Then He was put into a tomb.

But guess what? Good news! Jesus was alive again in three days. Just like He had said!

Some of Jesus' friends saw Him and talked to Him. They went into Galilee to tell the others, "Jesus has risen."

Based on Matthew 27:31-28:10

Questions for Discussion

1. Where did the soldiers put Jesus after He died?

2. Who was at the tomb when the women came?

3. What did the angel say?

story visual

What You Need
• duplicated page
• crayons

What to Do
1. Color the pictures.
2. To tell the story, hold the page so the children can see it easily. As you tell the story, point to that portion of the picture, including the cross.

More Ideas
1. Choose one child to be "Jesus." Have the children travel from one side of the room to the other. Help "Jesus" hide and then reappear to the others. Every time the children see "Jesus," have them clap their hands.
2. Use some bubble soap and a bubble wand to make bubbles, either in the classroom or outdoors. As the children watch the bubbles rise, say, **See how the bubbles rise? Jesus was in the tomb, but He said He would rise again. And He did!**

■ Died and ■ Rose Again

• Story Cross •

• Bulletin Board Poster •

He is risen. – Matthew 28:6

Poster Pointer

Tape a plastic page protector outside your classroom door. Above the page protector, place a sign that reads "This is what we are learning today." Slip the colored poster for the week into the page protector. Parents will know what their children are learning, and toddlers will be excited to see the new poster each week.

bulletin board

What You Need
- pattern on page 80
- construction paper or card stock
- clear, self-stick plastic
- straws
- tape

What to Do
1. Depending on how you want to use the poster (see ideas below and at left), enlarge, reduce or simply copy page 80 to fit your bulletin board space.
2. To use the poster as an in-class activity, copy the page for each child. Fold the page in half so that one scene is on the front and one scene is on the back. Tape the edges together. Help the children slip a straw inside the bottom and tape. Show the children how to turn the straw to see each scene.

■ Died and ■ Rose Again

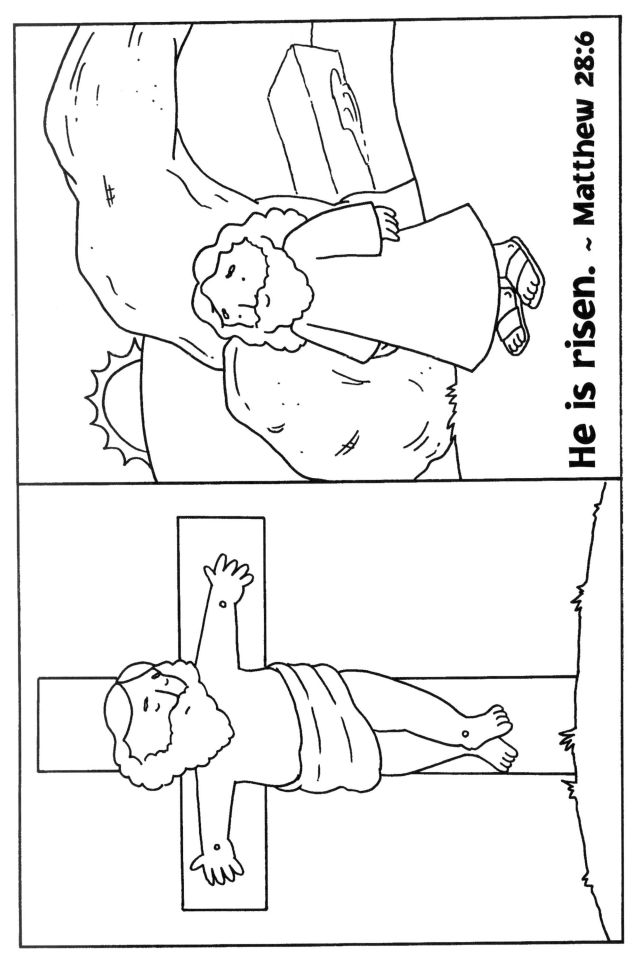

He is risen. ~ Matthew 28:6

• Who's in the Tomb? •

puzzle

What You Need
• duplicated page
• crayons

What to Do
1. Help the children color in the shapes with a star to find the angel.
2. Ask, **Who is in the tomb where Jesus was?**

■ **Died and** ■
Rose Again

81

• He Is Risen •

song/verse

What You Need
• duplicated page

What to Do

1. Teach the children the song "He Is Risen" to the tune of "Are You Sleeping?" As you sing the song with the children, rise on your toes to indicate that Jesus rose. Sing the song several times.

2. Say the "Happy-Clapping Verse" with the children, encouraging them to clap where appropriate.

He is Risen

He is risen,
He is risen.
From the tomb,
From the tomb.
Jesus Christ is risen.
Next, He'll go to heaven.
Praise the Lord.
Praise the Lord.

Happy-Clapping Verse

Happy, Happy.   *two claps*
Jesus' friends were happy.   *one clap*
Jesus arose from the tomb.
Jesus' friends were happy.   *one clap*

• Stand-up Jesus •

He has risen. ~ Matthew 28:6

craft

What You Need
- duplicated page
- crayons

What to Do
1. Before class, cut out a figure for each child. Cut it on the dashed lines, too, so the figure can stand.
2. Allow the children to color their pictures. While they work, say, **Jesus died on a cross, and then was put into a tomb. Three days later, Jesus rose from the tomb. Jesus has risen!**
3. Help the children fold the top half of the page back so the Jesus figure stands up.

■ **Died and** ■
Rose Again

• A Cross to Remember •

coloring

. . . .

What You Need
• duplicated page
• crayons

What to Do
1. While you tell the story, hold up a copy of the illustration for all the children to see.
2. Afterward, as the children color their pictures, discuss how happy we are that Jesus is risen.

Molly and Grandpa waited in the mall while Grandma shopped. "Let's walk around and look in some store windows," Grandpa said. "We can look at all the pretty things."

"I like to see the things in the windows, too," Molly said. She smiled at a funny picture. She waved at a teddy bear.

"What's that?" Molly asked. She was pointing to a white cross.

"That's a cross," Grandpa said. "Jesus died on a cross for everyone in the world. Then He was put in a tomb. In three days, Jesus rose again. God planned it that way."

Molly said, "I remember our Bible verse from Sunday school: 'He is risen.'"

"That's right," Grandpa said. "Would you like to have a cross to remember your Bible words?"

Molly smiled and chose the cross she wanted to take home. "Thank you," she told Grandpa as he paid for the cross.

■ Died and ■ Rose Again

• Happy Praises •
Tambourine

craft

What You Need
- duplicated page
- paper plates
- juice can lids
- construction paper
- stapler
- tape
- glue

What to Do
1. Before class, cut out the circle and a 2" x 10" strip of construction paper for each child.
2. Help the children glue the circle onto the outside of a plate. Fold the plate in half and staple the edges. Slip the juice lid inside before the last staple. (Cover the staples with tape to avoid injury.)
3. Help the children fold a construction paper strip in half, then staple it to the folded plate as a handle. (Cover staples with tape.)
4. Show how to hold the handle and shake it to make noise. Say, **We can make noise with our tambourines to celebrate that Jesus has risen!**

HE HAS RISEN

~ Matthew 28:6

■ **Died and** ■
Rose Again

craft

What You Need
- duplicated page
- paper towel tubes
- paper fasteners

What to Do
1. Before class, cut out the circle from the page for each child. Cut a slit on each solid line and cut out the center circle.
2. Help the children fold the flaps on the dashed lines (fold toward the picture).
3. Show how to slip the pinwheel over a thumb.
4. Help them hold their thumbs sideways and gently blow on the pinwheel. Say, **Your pinwheel says, "Jesus and Me....friends we will always be."**

More Ideas
Fasten the pinwheel to a paper towel tube with a paper fastener. Instead of cutting the hole in the center of the pinwheel, push the paper fastener through the center and through the tube. Hold onto the paper towel tube and blow on the pinwheel to make it spin.

■ Died and ■ Rose Again

• Jesus & Me Pinwheel •

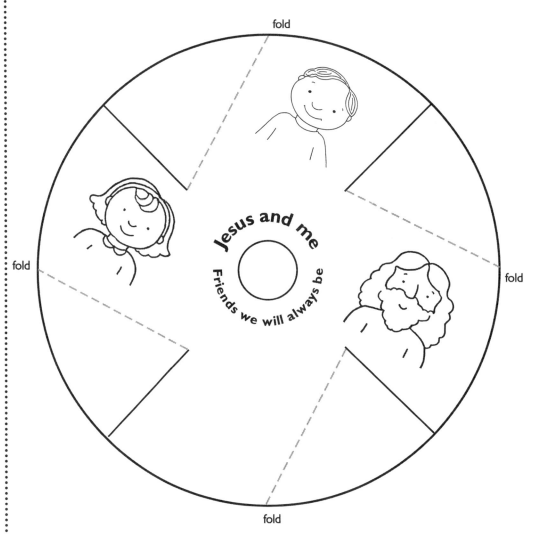

fold

fold

fold

fold

Jesus and me

Friends we will always be

• Out of the Tomb Game •

game

What You Need
• large box

What to Do
1. Use this activity to help the children understand the concept of Jesus rising from the tomb.
2. Place a large box in the center of the room.
3. Have some of the children crawl into the box.
4. Say, **Alex and Samantha are gone. We are so sad. Jason and Julie are gone, too. We are very sad that our friends are gone.**
5. Then have the children come out of the box. As they come out, say, **Oh, look! Alex, Samantha, Jason and Julie are risen. They are no longer in the tomb!**

■ Died and ■ Rose Again

■ ● Chapter 9 ● ■
More Friendly Activities

Jesus Is My Friend

Sing to the tune of "Good Night Ladies"

Jesus is my friend. *point to self*

point to self Jesus is my friend.

Jesus is my friend. *point to self*

He is your friend, too.

point to others

• Friendship Bracelets •

JESUS IS MY FRIEND!!

JESUS IS YOUR FRIEND!!

CUT

craft

What You Need
- duplicated page
- crayons
- tape

What to Do
1. Before class, cut out the two bracelets from the page for each child.
2. Have the children color their bracelets.
3. Help them place one bracelet around their wrist and tape it closed.
4. Help them tape the other bracelet into a circle.
5. Say, **This bracelet says, Jesus is your friend. Can you find someone to give your bracelet to?**

■ More ■

game

What You Need
- duplicated page
- envelopes
- crayons

What to Do
1. Make two copies of this page for each child. Before class, cut out the four squares from one of the copied pages. Leave the other page intact.
2. Help the children match the picture cards to the master page.
3. Discuss each picture. Say, for example, **Baby Jesus is God's Son. Jesus is our friend.**
4. Give each child an envelope in which to put the four picture cards.

• Memory Game •

• Cereal Counting Fun •

I will follow my friend Jesus.

5   6

4   7

3   8

2   9

1   10

What You Need
- duplicated page
- round cereal pieces

What to Do
1. Give each child a copy of the page, and 10 or more pieces of cereal.
2. Help the children count to 10 as they place their cereal pieces inside the circles on the page.
3. Have them say with you, **I will follow my friend, Jesus.**

■ More ■

What You Need
• duplicated page
• Jesus stickers

What to Do
1. Write each child's name on a chart.
2. Each week, let the child place a Jesus sticker on the chart.

• Attendance Charts •

Name: _____

MY FRIEND JESUS

• My Friend Jesus Book •

Jesus Is

My Friend

Name: _____

craft

What You Need
- this page and pp. 10, 20, 30, 41, 50, 61, 70 and 80, duplicated
- construction paper
- stapler

What to Do
1. Help the children glue each of the eight bulletin board pictures, plus this page, to construction paper.
2. Arrange the pages with this one on top.
3. Staple at the left edge. (Cover the staples with tape to avoid injury.)
4. Allow the children to color the pictures.

■ More ■

craft

What You Need
- duplicated page
- construction paper
- glue
- crayons
- yarn
- tape

What to Do

1. Before class, cut out the heart for each child.
2. Show how to glue the heart onto a sheet of construction paper.
3. Help the children draw a picture of their own face inside the child figure on the page.
4. Tape a loop of yarn at the top for hanging.

• Heart Plaque •

My friend Jesus loves me!

• Come with Me •

To come learn about
Jesus with me

You are invited

craft

What You Need
• duplicated page
• crayons

What to Do
1. Help the children fold the page into quarters to form a card.
2. While the children color their cards, say, **You can use this card to invite someone to come to church with you.**

■ **More** ■

craft

What You Need
- duplicated page
- crayons
- stapler
- tape

What to Do
1. Allow the children to color the front and back of Jesus' face.
2. Fold the illustration in half and staple it at the top and side only. Leave the bottom edge open. (Cover the staples with tape to avoid injury.)
3. Help the children slip the puppet onto their hands. Say, **You can tell others that Jesus is their friend by using your puppet.**

• My Friend Jesus Puppet •

Jesus is my friend.